# GALAXIES, GALAXIES!

New Edition

## BY GAIL GIBBONS

Holiday House / New York

# To Greta

Special thanks to Professor Edward Foley, teacher of astronomy, St. Michael's College, Colchester, Vermont, and Zhuo Chen, Ph.D. candidate, Department of Physics and Astronomy, University of Rochester, New York.

The Library of Congress has catalogued the prior edition as follows:
Gail Gibbons.
Galaxies, galaxies!/by Gail Gibbons.—1st ed.
p. cm.
ISBN-13: 978-0-8234-2002-5 (hardcover)
ISBN-10: 0-8234-2002-7 (hardcover)
1. Galaxies—Juvenile literature. I. Title.
QB857.3.G53 2006
523.1'12—dc22
2006002504

Second Edition
ISBN 978-0-8234-3964-5 (hardcover)
ISBN 978-0-8234-3965-2 (paperback)

A **STAR** is made up of burning gases that give off heat and light.

**O**n a clear, dark night, many stars light up the sky. A milky band of light glows from one end of the night sky to the other.

The milky band of light is called the Milky Way. It is made up of so many stars that they blur together when viewed from planet Earth.

The MILKY WAY

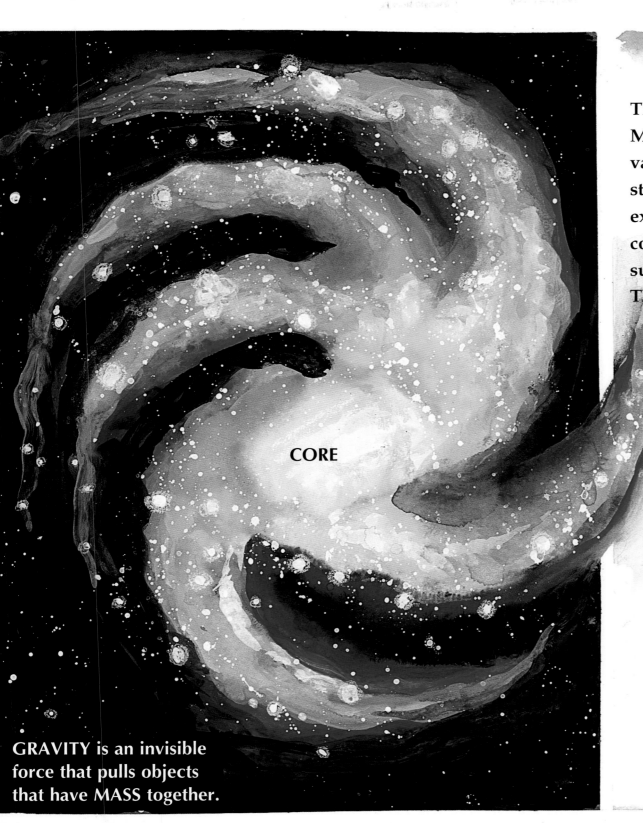

CORE

GRAVITY is an invisible
force that pulls objects
that have MASS together.

The Milky Way is part of the Milky Way Galaxy. In the galaxy's vast areas of dark space, there are stars, clouds of gases, and dust that exist around a nucleus, or central core. All of these things have substance to them called MASS. They are held together by gravity.

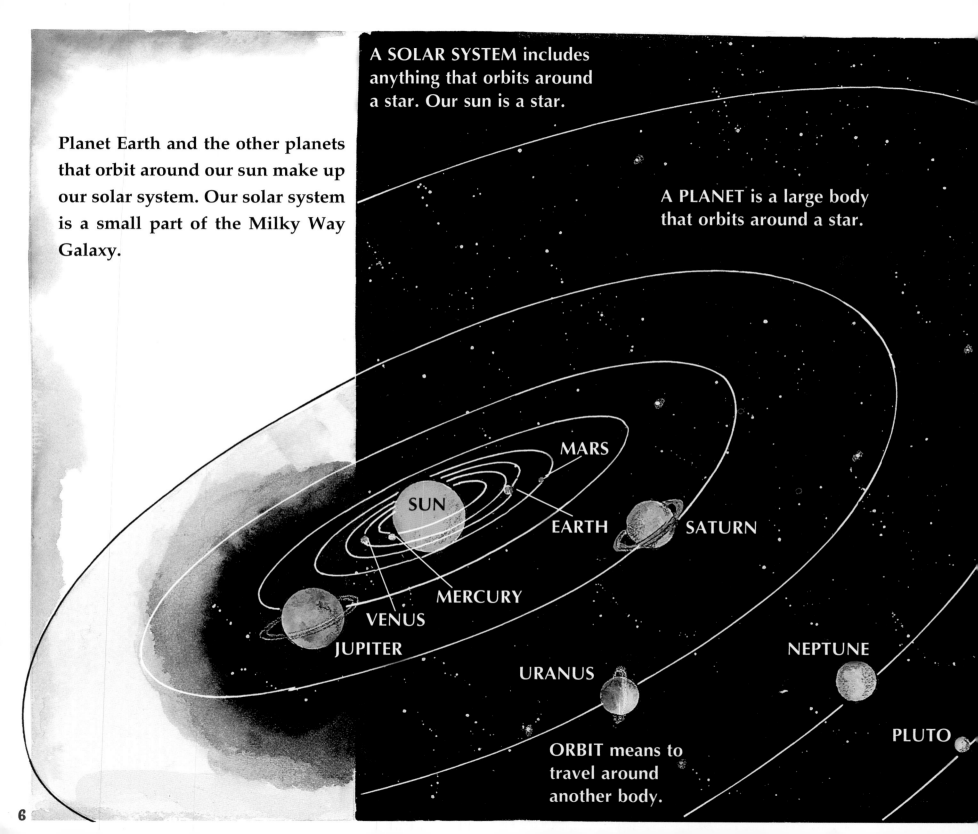

A SOLAR SYSTEM includes anything that orbits around a star. Our sun is a star.

Planet Earth and the other planets that orbit around our sun make up our solar system. Our solar system is a small part of the Milky Way Galaxy.

A PLANET is a large body that orbits around a star.

MARS

SUN

EARTH    SATURN

MERCURY

VENUS

JUPITER

URANUS

NEPTUNE

PLUTO

ORBIT means to travel around another body.

In ancient times people looked up at the night sky in wonder. They tried to understand what a star was and explain what the milky band was that spread across the night sky.

Ancient Greeks called it the "river of milk" and believed it was created by one of their gods when he was a baby.

Ancient civilizations tried creating maps of what they saw in the night sky. Today we call the study of stars and other celestial bodies astronomy.

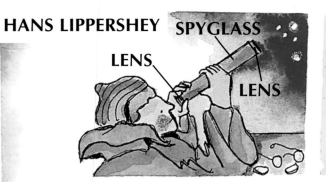

HANS LIPPERSHEY   SPYGLASS

LENS

LENS

**TELESCOPES are used to view distant objects.**

# REFRACTING TELESCOPE

In 1608, a Dutch eyeglass maker named Hans Lippershey put a lens at each end of a tube. He called the tube a spyglass because it made distant objects seem closer. One year later the Italian astronomer Galileo Galilei created stronger lenses, making objects in the sky appear even closer. Later his invention was called the refracting telescope.

**The OCULAR LENS magnifies.**

**The OBJECTIVE LENS bends light from stars into the telescope body.**

**With this kind of telescope, the observer looks directly at the stars and other objects.**

**GALILEO GALILEI**

# REFLECTING TELESCOPE

A CONCAVE MIRROR reflects light from stars back through the body of the telescope.

A MAGNIFYING LENS makes the images from the flat mirror larger.

A FLAT MIRROR reflects an image to a LENS.

In 1666, an Englishman named Isaac Newton invented the reflecting telescope. He placed two mirrors inside the telescope that bounced light back to a magnifying lens. His telescope was smaller but stronger than others had been.

**ISAAC NEWTON**

A REFLECTING TELESCOPE reflects an image by using two mirrors to view stars and other objects.

At first astronomers believed the Milky Way Galaxy was the entire universe. Over time, telescopes were made larger and their lenses stronger. The stars and other objects in the night sky became clearer. Many new discoveries could be made, such as those by the Herschel siblings, Caroline and Sir William, who observed previously unknown planets and comets.

The UNIVERSE is all of space and everything in it.

ANDROMEDA GALAXY

In the 1920s an American astronomer named Edwin Hubble discovered that a large group of stars called Andromeda (an·DRA·mu·duh) was not part of the Milky Way but actually another galaxy. This was the first time scientists could confirm that there was more than one galaxy in the universe. Hubble and other astronomers discovered more and more galaxies. Soon it was determined that there were billions and billions of galaxies. The known universe was getting bigger and bigger.

EDWIN HUBBLE

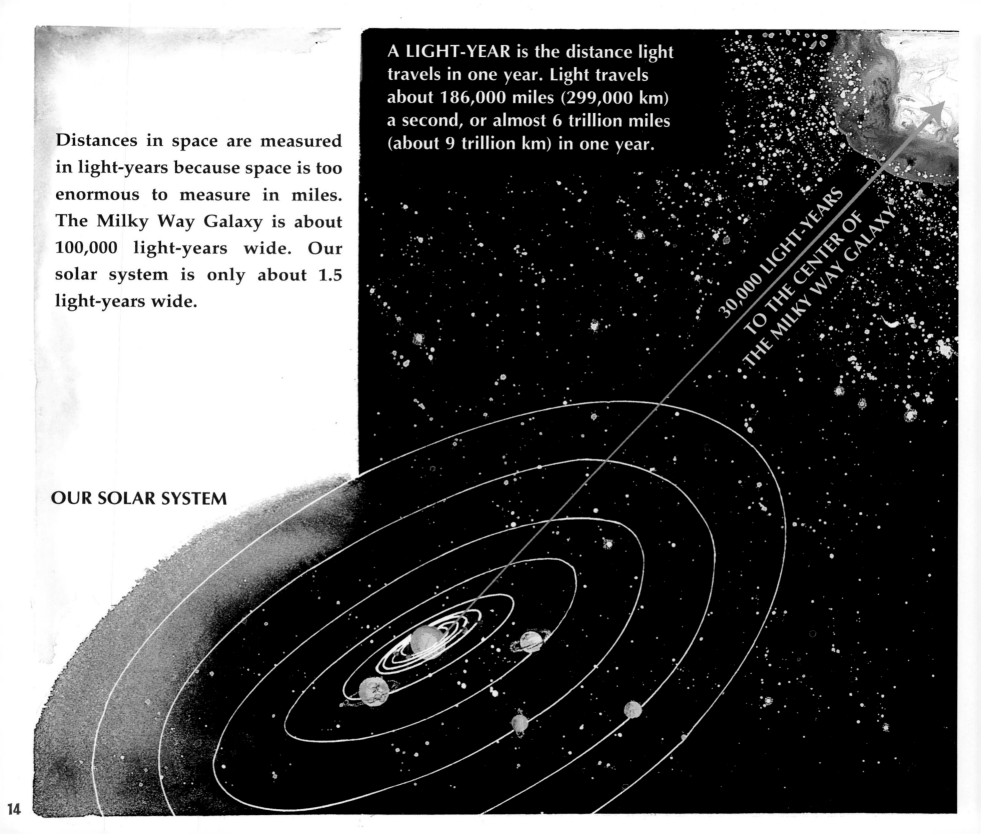

A **LIGHT-YEAR** is the distance light travels in one year. Light travels about 186,000 miles (299,000 km) a second, or almost 6 trillion miles (about 9 trillion km) in one year.

Distances in space are measured in light-years because space is too enormous to measure in miles. The Milky Way Galaxy is about 100,000 light-years wide. Our solar system is only about 1.5 light-years wide.

**30,000 LIGHT-YEARS TO THE CENTER OF THE MILKY WAY GALAXY**

**OUR SOLAR SYSTEM**

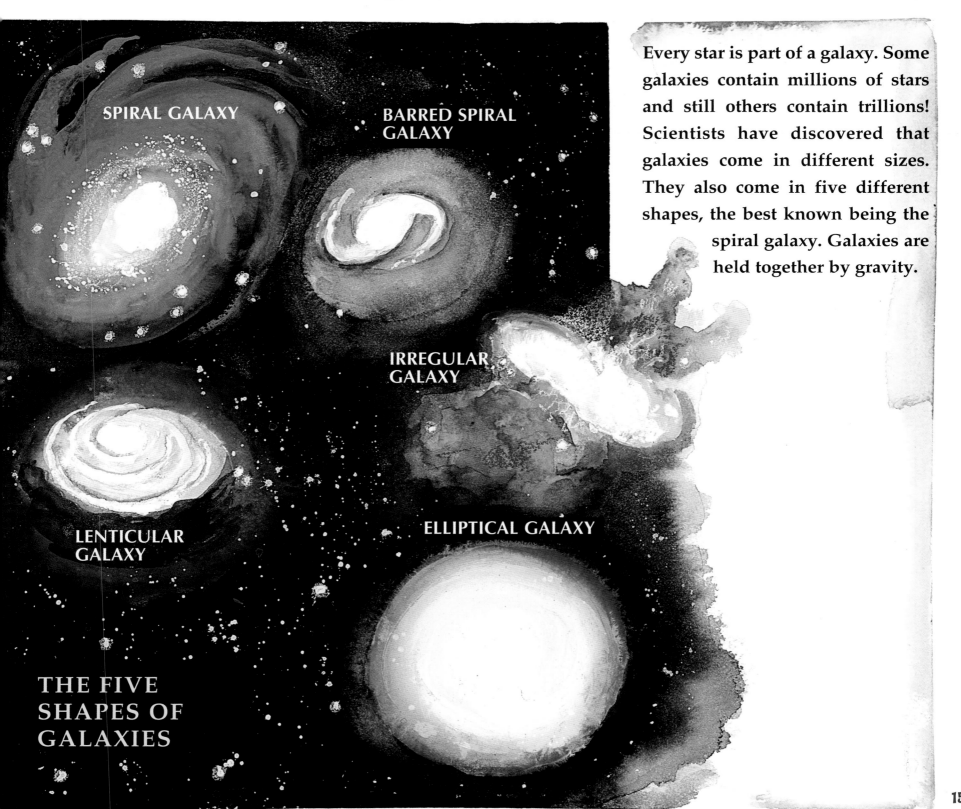

SPIRAL GALAXY

BARRED SPIRAL GALAXY

IRREGULAR GALAXY

LENTICULAR GALAXY

ELLIPTICAL GALAXY

THE FIVE SHAPES OF GALAXIES

Every star is part of a galaxy. Some galaxies contain millions of stars and still others contain trillions! Scientists have discovered that galaxies come in different sizes. They also come in five different shapes, the best known being the spiral galaxy. Galaxies are held together by gravity.

# SPIRAL GALAXY

The Milky Way Galaxy is a spiral galaxy. "Arms" of stars, gases, and dust spiral out from its center. Our solar system is within the arm of Orion.

## SOME "ARMS" IN OUR GALAXY

PERSEUS
(PURR·see·us) ARM

ORION (uh·RYE·un) ARM

OUR SOLAR SYSTEM

SWAN ARM

SAGITTARIUS
(sa·ju·TARE·ee·us) ARM

100,000
LIGHT-YEARS

CENTAURUS
(sen·TORE·us) ARM

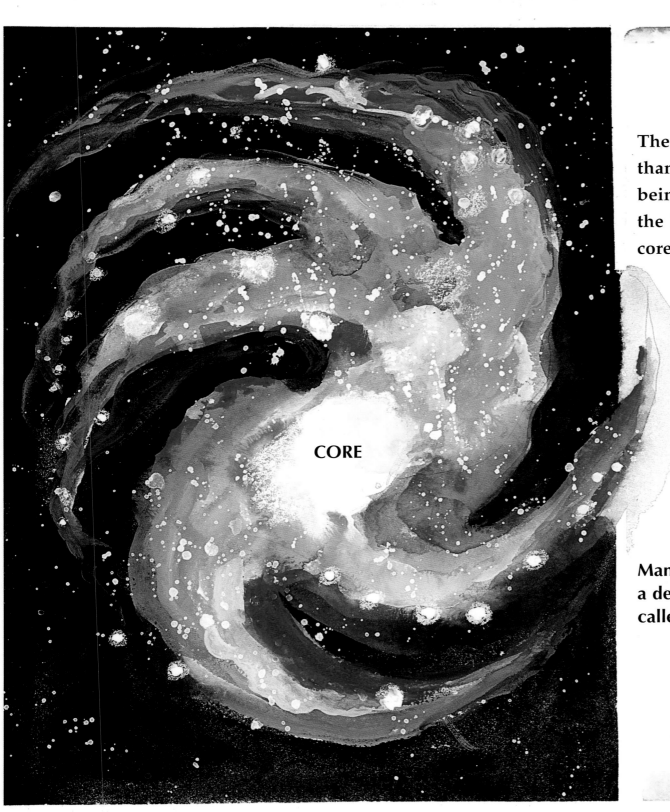

CORE

The Milky Way Galaxy has more than 100 billion stars, our sun being one of them. Everything in the Milky Way orbits around its core.

Many galaxies have a dense, central part called the CORE.

If you look at the Milky Way sideways, it appears sort of flat with a bulge in its core. The Milky Way is in a cluster of fifty-four galaxies.

**A CLUSTER is a group of galaxies.**

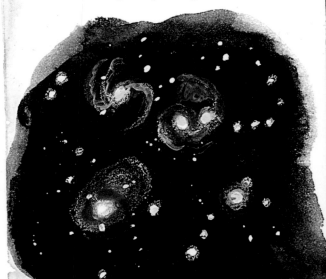

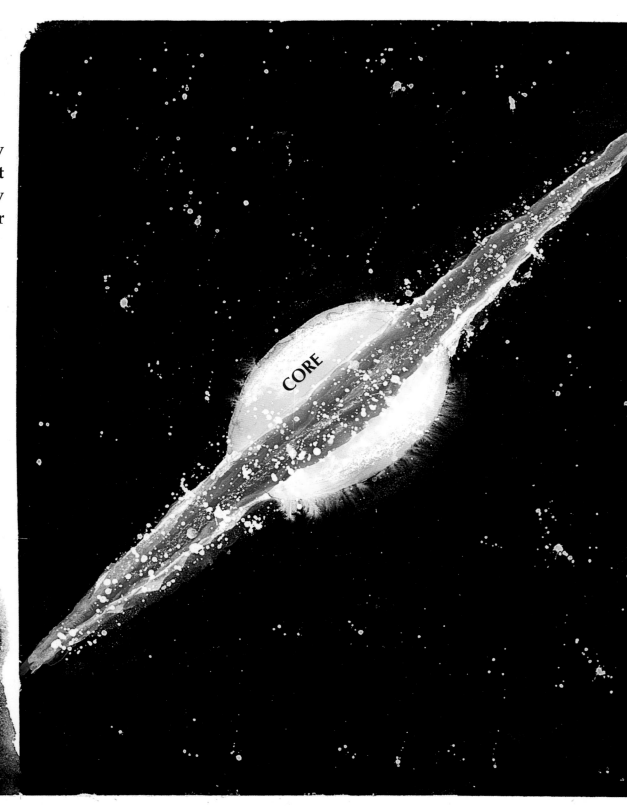

CORE

# BARRED SPIRAL GALAXY

**BAR-SHAPED CENTER**

**ARM**

**ARM**

A barred spiral galaxy has a dense, bar-shaped grouping of stars in its core. A spiral arm spins out from each end of the bar.

NGC (New General Catalog) is a record that provides the identification and location of galaxies.

The NGC 7479 GALAXY is a barred spiral galaxy.

# ELLIPTICAL GALAXY

An elliptical galaxy is ball-shaped. The largest elliptical galaxies are believed to be made up of trillions of stars.

The NGC 4881 GALAXY
is an elliptical galaxy.

# LENTICULAR GALAXY

A lenticular galaxy is shaped like a lens. Around the core of the galaxy are disks of stars and gases, giving it a lens-like, or lenticular, shape.

CORE

DISK OF STARS AND GASES

The NGC 2787 GALAXY is a lenticular galaxy.

# IRREGULAR GALAXY

This kind of galaxy doesn't have one kind of shape. Often irregular galaxies are small with lots of newly formed stars and bright gas clouds where new stars form. Some astronomers believe irregular galaxies form when two galaxies bump and merge into each other.

The NGC 2366 GALAXY is an irregular galaxy.

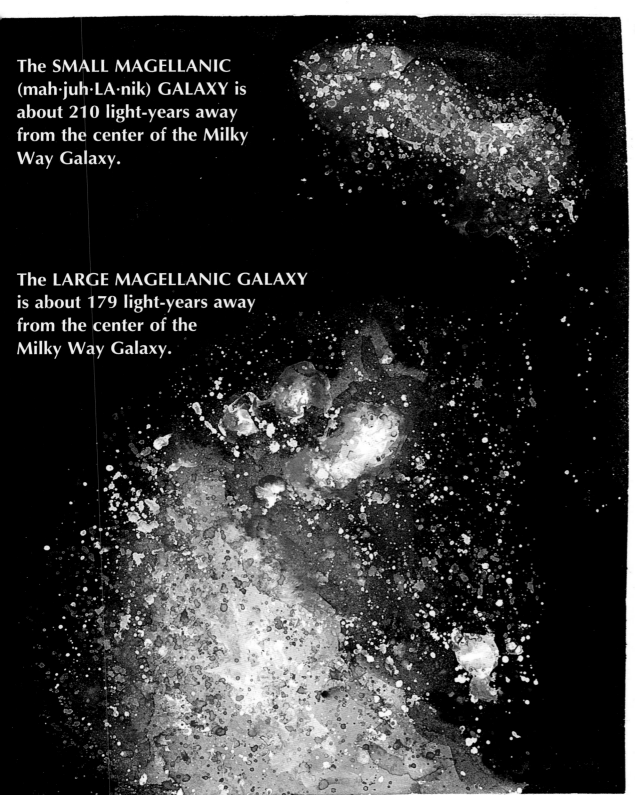

The **SMALL MAGELLANIC** (mah·juh·LA·nik) **GALAXY** is about 210 light-years away from the center of the Milky Way Galaxy.

The **LARGE MAGELLANIC GALAXY** is about 179 light-years away from the center of the Milky Way Galaxy.

There are two irregular galaxies that travel on the edge of the Milky Way Galaxy called the Large Magellanic Galaxy and Small Magellanic Galaxy. They are named for the Portuguese explorer Ferdinand Magellan. In 1519 he led the first expedition to sail around the world.

FERDINAND MAGELLAN

23

Inside galaxies some stars are being born and others are growing older and dying. Astronomers classify stars by their colors. Blue stars and white stars are the hottest and youngest. Yellow stars and orange stars are the coolest and oldest. Our sun is a middle-aged yellow star.

**Our SUN should heat Earth for another 5 billion years.**

BLUE

YELLOWISH WHITE

YELLOW

BLUISH WHITE

ORANGE

RED

WHITE

Today astronomers are able to discover and study even more galaxies. Observatories have huge reflecting telescopes that gather more light and allow observers to see deeper into the universe. Many observatories are built on the tops of mountains, where the air is clear and there are no distracting city lights.

OBSERVATORY

Galaxies can give off different kinds of energy that help us discover even more about the universe. Some of these are X-rays, gamma rays, ultraviolet radiation, and radio waves. Radio waves transmit sounds. Ground-based radio telescopes use giant antennas to tune in to radio waves coming from faraway stars and galaxies. More discoveries are made this way.

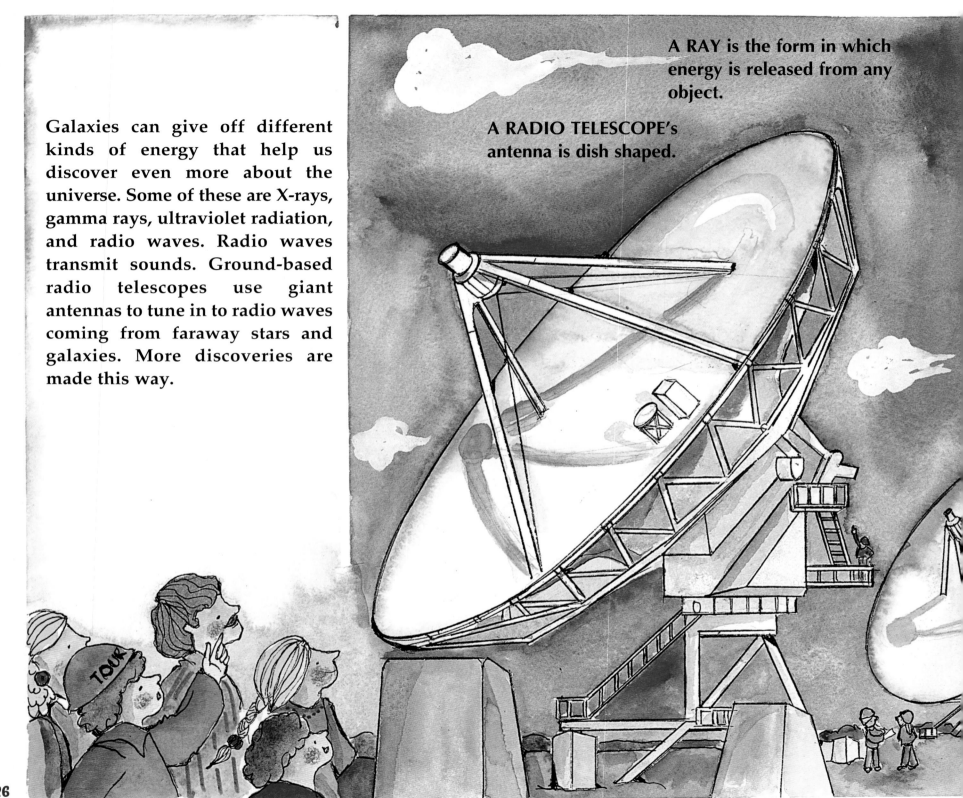

A RAY is the form in which energy is released from any object.

A RADIO TELESCOPE's antenna is dish shaped.

**HUBBLE SPACE TELESCOPE**

There are telescopes in space too. The largest, a reflecting telescope named after Edwin Hubble, was launched in 1990. It is about as big as a school bus. Because it orbits above Earth's atmosphere, it can see deep into the universe. The Hubble can see galaxies billions of light-years away.

The ATMOSPHERE is a layer of air surrounding Earth.

Unmanned space probes have
been launched into deep space.
The probes are loaded with
cameras and other equipment for
exploring.

VOYAGER 1

They transmit their discoveries back to astronomers on Earth.

Currently astronomers know there are more than 100 billion galaxies in the universe, with many left to be discovered.

There are still more being formed and even more yet to be formed.

# GALAXIES . . .

Most stars that are visible to the naked eye are within a few hundred light-years of Earth.

The largest radio telescope in the world is called the FAST radio telescope. It is 1,640 feet (500 m) wide and is located in China.

Our sun is only 8 light-minutes from Earth.

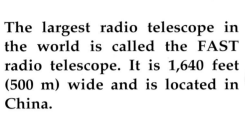

Some observatories give tours to help people learn what astronomers do.

Our solar system takes about 220 million years to complete a trip around the center, or core, of the Milky Way.

Planetariums offer lectures about stars and galaxies. Images are projected on the inside of a domed ceiling. Some scientists, such as Neil deGrasse Tyson, also give lectures about stars and galaxies on TV and online.

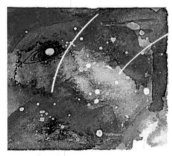

Galaxies are given names by the people who discover them.

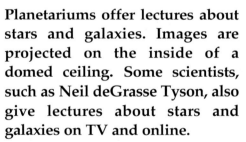

It is fun to look up at the wonders of the night sky.

The largest optical telescope in the world is the Great Canary Telescope in the Canary Islands.